Bruce Springsteen

101 Questions To Test Your Knowledge
Of This Incredibly Successful Musician

By Colin Carter

Bruce Springsteen Quiz

This book contains one hundred and one informative and entertaining trivia questions with multiple choice answers. With 101 questions, some easy, some more demanding, this entertaining book will really test your knowledge of |Bruce Springsteen.

You will be quizzed on a wide range of topics associated with Bruce for you to test yourself; with questions on his early days, songs, lyrics, achievements, awards and much more, guaranteeing you a truly fun, educational experience.

This quiz book will provide entertainment for fans of all ages and will certainly test your knowledge of this world-famous musician. The book is packed with information and is a must-have for all true Springsteen fans, wherever you live in the world.

Published by Glowworm Press
glowwormpress.com

Disclaimer

All Rights Reserved. No part of this publication may be reproduced, distributed, or transmitted in any form or by any means, including photocopying, without the written permission of the publisher; with the exception of reviews written for a blog, website, magazine or newspaper and certain other non-commercial uses permitted by copyright law. Product names referred to within this publication are the property of their respective trademark holders. This book is unofficial and is not authorised by the aforementioned interests. This book is licensed for your personal enjoyment only. The image on the cover of this book is either the property of the author/publisher or is used under appropriate licenses or agreements. Any queries please email support@glowwormpress.com

ACKNOWLEDGEMENTS

My friend Paul simply adores Bruce Springsteen.

As a writer, I thought I would write a book on Bruce for him to test himself and to see how much he really knows about the legend that is Springsteen.

Of course, I know that Springsteen has millions of fans and that I should write the book for every one of them, not just him.

So I did! This book is for all you wonderful Bruce Springsteen fans – wherever you live in the world.

I hope you enjoy it.

Colin Carter

OK, Here goes. Here is the first set of questions.

Q1. When was Bruce Springsteen born?
A. September 23, 1949
B. September 25, 1949
C. September 27, 1949
D. September 29, 1949

Q2. Where was Bruce Springsteen born?
A. New Hampshire
B. New Jersey
C. New Mexico
D. New York

Q3. What are Springsteen's middle names?
A. Francis Joseph
B. Frank Joseph
C. Frederick Joseph
D. Forest Joseph

Q4. How many siblings does Bruce have?
A. One
B. Two
C. Three
D. Four

Q5. What is the name of Bruce's current (second) wife?
A. Patti Austin
B. Patti Boyd
C. Patti Cake
D. Patti Scialfa

Q6. Where did he meet his current wife?
A. At a concert
B. At a music festival
C. On the set of a music video
D. In a recording studio

Q7. When did they marry?
A. 1988
B. 1989
C. 1990
D. 1991

Q8. What is the name of Bruce Springsteen's first child?
A. Earl
B. Edgar
C. Elijah
D. Evan

Q9. How many children does Bruce have?
A. Two
B. Three
C. Four
D. Five

Q10. Which was the first musical instrument Bruce learnt to play?
A. Banjo
B. Guitar
C. Mandolin
D. Ukelele

Here is the first set of answers. If you get seven or more right, you are doing well, but the questions will get harder!

A1. Bruce Springsteen was born on September 23, 1949. His star sign is Virgo. Virgos are often described as practical and detail-oriented, traits that can be seen in Springsteen's meticulous approach to his music.

A2. Bruce Springsteen was born in Long Branch, New Jersey. His experiences in Freehold significantly influenced his songwriting.

A3. His middle names are Frederick Joseph. His full name is Bruce Frederick Joseph Springsteen.

A4. He has one sibling, a younger sister named Pamela. She is a photographer and actress.

A5. His current wife is Patti Scialfa. They have been married since 1991 and have collaborated on several musical projects.

A6. He met Patti Scialfa on the set of a music video. Scialfa was hired as a backup singer for Springsteen's "Born to Run" tour.

A7. Bruce Springsteen and Patti Scialfa married in 1991. Their wedding was a private ceremony held at their home.

A8. Bruce's first child is named Evan. He was born in 1990.

A9. Bruce Springsteen has three children. They are Evan, Jessica, and Sam.

A10. Bruce first learned to play the guitar. He initially taught himself to play and later received formal lessons. That's a nice easy one to finish the first block of questions.

Here is the next set of questions.

Q11. What color eyes does Bruce have?
A. Blue
B. Brown
C. Green
D. Hazel

Q12. What color hair does Bruce have?
A. Black
B. Blonde
C. Brown
D. Red

Q13. How tall is Bruce?
A. 5 feet 5 inches
B. 5 feet 7 inches
C. 5 feet 9 inches
D. 5 feet 11 inches

Q14. What is Bruce's nickname?
A. The Boss
B. The Chief
C. The Duke
D. The King

Q15. What was Bruce's first job?
A. Construction worker
B. Factory worker
C. Gas station attendant
D. Music teacher

Q16. How many tattoos has Bruce got?

A. None
B. One
C. Two
D. Three

Q17. Which year did Bruce release his debut album?
A. 1971
B. 1972
C. 1973
D. 1974

Q18. What is the name of the primary backing band for Bruce?
A. The B Street Band
B. The C Street Band
C. The D Street Band
D. The E Street Band

Q19. Who was Bruce's first manager?
A. George Theiss
B. Jon Landau
B. Mike Appel
D. Steve Van Zandt

Q20. What is the name of Bruce's first single?
A. Blinded by the Light
B. Born to Run
C. Dancing in the Dark
D. Thunder Road

Here is the latest set of answers.

A11. Bruce has brown eyes. They are sometimes referred to as amber.

A12. Bruce's natural hair color is brown, though it has grayed with age. His iconic look includes his tousled, often messy hair.

A13. Bruce is commonly recorded as being 5 feet 9 inches tall. His height adds to his commanding presence on stage.

A14. Bruce's nickname is "The Boss." This moniker reflects his authoritative presence and leadership in the music industry.

A15. Bruce's first job was as a construction worker. He took on various odd jobs to support himself while pursuing his music career.

A16. Bruce has no tattoos. Although, he is known for his classic rock and roll image, he has chosen not to cover his body with tattoos.

A17. Bruce's debut album, "Greetings from Asbury Park, N.J.", was released in January 1973. This album marked the beginning of his successful music career.

A18. The E Street Band has been the primary backing band for Bruce's performing and recording career.

A19. Bruce's first manager was Mike Appel. Appel played a crucial role in launching Springsteen's career.

A20. Bruce's first single was "Blinded by the Light". This song was originally written and recorded for his debut album and was not a hit single, but it gained significant attention after being covered by Manfred Mann's Earth Band, albeit in a much re-arranged version.

Here is the next set of questions.

Q21. What was the name of the first record label Bruce signed to?
A. Columbia Records
B. Epic Records
C. RCA Records
D. Warner Bros. Records

Q22. What is the name of Bruce's first album?
A. Born to Run
B. Greetings from Asbury Park, N.J.
C. Nebraska
D. The River

Q23. When was this debut album released?
A. 1972
B. 1973
C. 1974
D. 1975

Q24. What is the name of Bruce's second album?
A. Born in the U.S.A.
B. Darkness on the Edge of Town
C. The River
D. The Wild, the Innocent & the E Street Shuffle

Q25. What is the name of Bruce's third album?
A. Born to Run
B. Darkness on the Edge of Town
C. Nebraska
D. The River

Q26. When did Bruce first reach the top of the US singles chart?
A. 1980
B. 1982
C. 1984
D. 1986

Q27. Which was Bruce's first number one album in the US?
A. Born in the U.S.A.
B. Born to Run
C. Darkness on the Edge of Town
D. The River

Q28. How many records has Bruce sold in total?
A. 25 million
B. 50 million
C. 100 million
D. 150 million

Q29. What is Bruce's vocal range classified as?
A. Baritone
B. Bass
C. Tenor
D. Alto

Q30. What was the title of Bruce's debut solo tour?
A. Born to Run Tour
B. Greetings from Asbury Park Tour
C. Nebraska Tour
D. The River Tour

Here are the answers to the latest set of questions.

A21. Bruce's first record label was Columbia Records. He signed with Columbia in 1972, and this partnership led to a number of album releases.

A22. Bruce's debut album was called "Greetings from Asbury Park, N.J.". This album was critical in establishing him as a significant new artist.

A23. Bruce's debut album "Greetings from Asbury Park, N.J." was released in 1973. It introduced his distinctive sound and lyrical style to the public.

A24. Bruce's second album is "The Wild, the Innocent & the E Street Shuffle". Released in 1973, it further established his reputation with its eclectic and energetic sound.

A25. Bruce's third album is "Born to Run". Released in 1975, this album marked a major breakthrough in his career and is considered one of the greatest rock albums of all time.

A26. Bruce first reached the top of the US singles chart in 1984 with "Dancing in the Dark". This song was on the "Born in the U.S.A." album.

A27. Bruce's first number one album in the US was "The River". Released in 1980, it marked a significant commercial milestone in his career.

A28. Bruce has sold over 150 million records worldwide. His extensive discography and enduring popularity have made him one of the world's best-selling artists.

A29. Bruce's vocal range is classified as baritone. His voice is known for its gritty and powerful quality, which complements his rock and roll style.

A30. Bruce's debut solo tour was called the "Greetings from Asbury Park Tour". This tour supported his first album and was crucial in building his early fan base.

Here is the next set of questions.

Q31. Who directed the music video for "Dancing in the Dark"?
A. Brian De Palma
B. David Fincher
C. John Sayles
D. Steven Spielberg

Q32. Who does Springsteen pull on stage in the "Dancing in the Dark" music video?
A. Jennifer Aniston
B. Courtney Cox
C. Lisa Kudrow
D. Drea de Matteo

Q33. What is Bruce seen doing during the video for "I'm on Fire"?
A. Driving a car
B. Performing on stage
C. Sitting in a small room
D. Walking down a city street

Q34. Where is Bruce seen meeting his old friends in the music video for "Glory Days,"?
A. At a baseball game
B. At a high school reunion
C. In a bar
D. On a city street

Q35. What significant event is depicted in the music video for "Streets of Philadelphia"?
A. A funeral procession

B. A protest march
C. A street performance
D. A wedding

Q36. Who is featured alongside Bruce in the music video for "Tunnel of Love"?
A. Dolly Parton
B. Jessica Springsteen
C. Julianne Phillips
D. Patti Scialfa

Q37. What is the visual style of the music video for "My Hometown"?
A. Animated sequences
B. Black and white
C. Colorful and vibrant
D. Documentary-style footage

Q38. What is Bruce seen doing at the end of the music video for "Rosalita (Come Out Tonight)"?
A. Dancing with the audience
B. Driving a car
C. Performing on top of a car
D. Walking through a crowd

Q39. What is the central theme of the music video for "The River"?
A. Adventure and exploration
B. Celebration and joy
C. Domestic struggle and hardship
D. Youth and rebellion

Q40. Which Christmas song is most closely associated with Springsteen?
A. All I Want For Christas Is You
B. Last Christmas
C. Rockin' Around The Christmas Tree
D. Santa Claus Is Comin' To Town

Here is the latest set of answers.

A31. The music video for "Dancing in the Dark" was directed by Brian De Palma.

A32. The iconic video for "Dancing in the Dark" features a young Courteney Cox. She appears as a fan pulled on stage by Springsteen and then the two dance together on stage.

A33. In the video for "I'm on Fire," Bruce Springsteen is seen driving a convertible. This car symbolizes freedom and escape, themes central to the song's narrative.

A34. In the music video for "Glory Days," Bruce is seen meeting his old friends in a bar. The setting captures the nostalgic and celebratory nature of the song's theme about reminiscing past experiences.

A35. The music video for "Streets of Philadelphia" depicts a funeral procession. The somber and reflective nature of the video matches the song's exploration of the struggles faced by people suffering from AIDS.

A36. Patti Scialfa is featured alongside Bruce in the music video for "Tunnel of Love." Their on-screen chemistry complements the song's themes of romance and relationship complexity.

A37. The visual style of the music video for "My Hometown" is predominantly black and white. This choice enhances the song's nostalgic and reflective tone, focusing on the themes of change and memory.

A38. At the end of the music video for "Rosalita (Come Out Tonight)," Bruce is seen performing on top of a car. This energetic finale captures the exuberance and joy of the song's live performance.

A39. The central theme of the music video for "The River" is domestic struggle and hardship. The video depicts the difficult realities of working-class life, reflecting the song's poignant lyrics about economic hardship and personal struggles.

A40. "Santa Claus is Comin' to Town" is the Christmas song most closely associated with Springsteen. It was recorded back in 1975 and has been a concert favorite, particularly in November and December with the audience often encouraged to sing along.

Here is the next set of questions.

Q41. Which song starts with the lyrics "In the day we sweat it out on the streets of a runaway American dream"?
A. Badlands
B. Born To Run
C. Glory Days
D. Jungleland

Q42. Which song begins with "The screen door slams, Mary's dress sways"?
A. Dancing in the Dark
B. I'm on Fire
C. The River
D. Thunder Road

Q43. What song opens with the line "I was bruised and battered; I couldn't tell what I felt"?
A. Nebraska
B. Streets of Philadelphia
C. The Ghost of Tom Joad
D. The River

Q44. Which song starts with "I hold you in my arms as the band plays"?
A. Brilliant Disguise
B. Dancing in the Dark
C. Hungry Heart
D. Tunnel of Love

Q45. Which song begins with the lyrics "On a rattlesnake speedway in the Utah desert"?

A. Badlands
A. Jungleland
C. The Promised Land
D. The River

Q46. Which song starts with "Men walking along the railroad tracks going someplace and there's no going back"?
A. Born in the U.S.A.
B. Nebraska
C. The Ghost of Tom Joad
D. The River

Q47. What song opens with "Friday night and a guy's fresh out of work, talking 'bout the weekend, scrubbing off the dirt"?
A. Dancing in the Dark
B. Hungry Heart
C. Tougher Than the Rest
D. Working on the Highway

Q48. What song opens with "Hey, little girl, is your Daddy home. Did he go away and leave you all alone"?
A. Dancing in the Dark
B. I'm on Fire
C. The River
D. Tunnel of Love

Q49. What song opens with "Got a wife and kids in Baltimore, Jack. I went out for a ride and I never went back"?
A. Dancing in the Dark
B Hungry Heart

C. I'm on Fire
D. Prove It All Night

Q50. What song starts with "I had a friend, was a big baseball player"?
A. Badlands
B. Cover Me
C. Glory Days
D. Secret Garden

Here are the answers to the opening lyrics questions.

A41. The song that starts with the lyrics "In the day we sweat it out on the streets of a runaway American dream" is "Born to Run". These opening lines set the stage for the anthemic and iconic rock track that celebrates youthful ambition and escape.

A42. The song that begins with "The screen door slams, Mary's dress sways, Like a vision she dances across the porch, as the radio plays" is "Thunder Road". This opening paints a vivid picture of a small-town scene, setting up the narrative of the song.

A43. The song that opens with "I was bruised and battered; I couldn't tell what I felt" is "Streets of Philadelphia". This introduction reflects the song's themes of struggle and disillusionment.

A44. The song that starts with "I hold you in my arms as the band plays, what are those words whispered, baby just as you turned away" is "Brilliant Disguise". The opening lyrics introduce the theme of questioning and self-reflection in relationships.

A45. The song that begins with the lyrics "On a rattlesnake speedway in the Utah desert" is "The Promised Land". These words set the scene for a narrative exploring themes of struggle and redemption.

A46. The song that starts with "Men walking along the railroad tracks, going someplace and there's no going back" is "The Ghost of Tom Joad". These lyrics reflect the song's focus on poverty and social injustice. The title of the song is a reference to John Steinbeck's novel *The Grapes of Wrath*, and the migration of the Joad family from Oklahoma to California.

A47. The song that opens with "Friday night and a guy's fresh out of work, talking 'bout the weekend, scrubbing off the dirt" is "Working on the Highway". This introduction captures the daily grind and labor of the working class.

A48. The song that opens with "Hey, little girl, is your Daddy home. Did he go away and leave you all alone" is "I'm on Fire". These opening lines sets a tone of desire and concern.

A49. "Got a wife and kids in Baltimore, Jack. I went out for a ride, and I never went back" are the first lines to "Hungry Heart". The opening lines reflect themes of loneliness and longing.

A50. "I had a friend, was a big baseball player" is from Glory Days. It introduces a nostalgic theme, recalling a past friend who was a star athlete, setting the stage for a reflection on how time has passed and how people often reminisce about their youthful successes.

Here is the next set of questions.

Q51. Which album includes the song "Tenth Avenue Freeze-Out"?
A. Born to Run
B. Devils & Dust
C. Nebraska
D. The Ghost of Tom Joad

Q52. Which of these songs is featured on the album "The River"?
A. Born in the U.S.A.
B. Dancing in the Dark
C. Hungry Heart
D. Thunder Road

Q53. Which album features the song "Dancing in the Dark"?
A. Born in the U.S.A.
B. Darkness on the Edge of Town
C. Lucky Town
D. Nebraska

Q54. Which song is included on the album "Darkness on the Edge of Town"?
A. Atlantic City
B. Badlands
C. Rosalita (Come Out Tonight)
D. Fade Away

Q55. Which album includes the song "Lonesome Day"?
A. The Ghost of Tom Joad
B. The Rising

C. Tunnel of Love
D. Working on a Dream

Q56. Which of these songs is on the album "Nebraska"?
A. Atlantic City
B. Jungleland
C. Prove It All Night
D. Thunder Road

Q57. Which of these songs is included in the album "Working on a Dream"?
A. Dead Man Walking
B. Outlaw Pete
C. Spare Parts
D. War

Q58. Which album includes the track "Rosalita (Come Out Tonight)"?
A. American Beauty
B. Greetings from Astbury Park, NJ
C. The Wild, The Innocent & The E Street Shuffle
D. Tunnel of Love

Q59. Which album features the song "Radio Nowhere"?
A. Devils & Dust
B. Letter To You
C. Magic
D. The Ghost of Tom Joad

Q60. Which album features the song "Brilliant Disguise"?

A. Lucky Town
B. Tunnel of Love
C. Western Stars
D. Wrecking Ball

Here is the latest set of answers.

A51. The album "Born to Run" includes the song "Tenth Avenue Freeze-Out." The album features multiple styles and took an incredible 18 months to record, including a reported 6 months on the title track alone.

A52. "Hungry Heart" is featured on the album "The River". The song, which became a major hit, showcases Springsteen's ability to blend personal storytelling with a catchy, anthemic sound. This track, with its upbeat tempo and catchy chorus, became one of Springsteen's biggest hits.

A53. "Dancing in the Dark" is featured on the album "Born in the U.S.A." The song's catchy melody and reflective lyrics highlight Springsteen's skill in blending introspection with mainstream appeal.

A54. "Badlands" is included on the album "Darkness on the Edge of Town". This powerful track is known for its driving rhythm and evocative lyrics about struggle and resilience.

A55. "Lonesome Day" is on the album "The Rising" This album, reflecting on the aftermath of 9/11, offers a poignant and uplifting response to the tragedy.

A56. "Atlantic City" is featured on the from the album "Nebraska". The album, known for its raw and stripped-down acoustics sound, features this track as a prime example of its intimate and haunting quality.

A57. "Outlaw Pete" is the first song on the album "Working on a Dream". This song tells the life story of a notorious outlaw, blending themes of redemption, the consequences of a violent life, and the inescapable nature of one's past.

A58. "Rosalita (Come Out Tonight)" is included in the album "The Wild, The Innocent & The E Street Shuffle". This energetic and exuberant song is a highlight of the album, showcasing Springsteen's storytelling and performance skills.

A59 "Radio Nowhere" is on the album "Magic". This is a rock song expressing a sense of alienation and longing for genuine human connection.

A60. "Brilliant Disguise" is on the album "Tunnel of Love". This song is about the complexities of relationships, exploring themes of doubt, self-deception, and the fear of not truly knowing oneself or one's partner.

Here is the next set of questions.

Q61. Who was the producer of the "Born in the U.S.A." album?
A. Brendan O'Brien
B. Jon Landau
C. Steve Lillywhite
D. Steve Van Zandt

Q62. Who was the co-producer, along with Springsteen, of the "Wrecking Ball " album?
A. Brendan O'Brien
B. Clive Davis
C. Ron Aniello
D. Steve Van Zandt

Q63. Who did Bruce collaborate with on the song "Because The Night"?
A. Aretha Franklin
B. Melissa Etheridge
C. Patti Smith
D. Shania Twain

Q64. Which song includes the line "You can hide beneath your covers and study your pain"?
A. Born to Run
B. The Promise
C. The River
D. Thunder Road

Q65. What was the name of the song that Natalie Cole covered and a huge hit with in 1988?
A. Blue Buick

B. Green Pontiac
C. Pink Cadillac
D. Red Thunderbird

Q66. What was the name of the Springsteen written song The Pointer Sisters had a hit with in 1978?
A. Air
B. Earth
C. Fire
D. Water

Q67. Who did Springsteen originally write the song for?
A. Elvis Presley
B. Jerry Lee Lewis
C. Michael Jackson
D. Prince

Q68. What is Springsteen's official website address?
A. brucespringsteen.com
B. brucespringsteen.net
C. brucespringsteen.org
D. .brucespringsteenmusic.com

Q69. What is Springsteen's official Instagram account?
A. @bruce_springsteen
B. @bruce_springsteen_official
C. @springsteen_bruce
D. @theboss

Q70. What is Springsteen's official X (formerly Twitter) account?
A. @BossSpringsteen

B. @BruceSpringsteen
C. @Springsteen
D. @TheRealSpringsteen

Here is the latest set of answers.

A61. Jon Landau was the producer of the iconic "Born in the U.S.A." album. Landau's influence and production work played a crucial role in shaping the album's sound.

A62. The co-producer of the "Wrecking Ball" album was Ron Aniello. He was co-producer or sole producer on a number of Bruce's later albums too, including High Hopes, Western Stars, Letter to You and Only the Strong Survive. Give yourself a bonus point if you knew some of that.

A63. Bruce collaborated with Patti Smith on the song "Because the Night". The song has co-writing credits and it went on to become her best ever selling song. The song has been covered a number of times since.

A64. Bruce sings the line "You can hide beneath your covers and study your pain" in the song "Thunder Road". This track is an iconic anthem about hope, escape, and the pursuit of a better life, capturing the spirit of youthful ambition and the desire for freedom.

A65. "Pink Cadillac" was written by Bruce in 1983 and it was the B side to "Dancing in the Dark". Natalie Cole covered the song in 1988 and it became a top ten hit for her. If you don't know Bruce's original, it is worth tracking down on YouTube. It has a wonderful backbeat.

A66. "Fire" was written by Bruce in 1977, and it went on to be a huge hit for The Pointer Sisters when it was released as a single in 1978.

A67. Bruce originally wrote "Fire" for Elvis Presley, and a demo of the song was sent to him. Unfortunately, Elvis died before the demo arrived!

A68. Springsteen's official website address is brucespringsteen.net. The site provides updates on his music, tours, and other relevant news.

A69. Springsteen's official Instagram account is @springsteen_bruce. This account features updates on his music, performances, and personal insights.

A70. Springsteen's official X account is @springsteen. This platform provides its millions of followers with the latest news.

Here is the next set of questions.

Q71. What was the title of Bruce Springsteen's autobiography?
A. Born to Live
B. Born to Love
C. Born to Rock
D. Born to Run

Q72. Which of these songs did Bruce open with at the Super Bowl XLIII halftime show in Tampa in 2009?
A. Born to Run
B. Glory Days
C. Tenth Avenue Freeze-Out
D. Working on a Dream

Q73. Which of these four albums was released first?
A. Darkness on the Edge of Town
B. Nebraska
C. The Rising
D. Tunnel of Love

Q74. Which year was the album "Magic" released?
A. 2005
B. 2007
C. 2009
D. 2011

Q75. What year did the album "Wrecking Ball" come out?
A. 2010
B. 2012
C. 2014

D. 2016

Q76. Who did Bruce sell his music rights to in 2021?
A. Amazon
B. Apple
C. Sony
D. Universal

Q77. Which song from the album "Nebraska" was based on serial killer Charles Starkweather?
A. Atlantic City
B. Highway Patrolman
C. Nebraska
D. State Trooper

Q78. Which of these has never been a member of the E Street Band?
A. David Sancious
B. Jon Lyon
C. Nils Lofgren
D. Vini Lopez

Q79. What confession did Bruce make in his hit stage show "Springsteen on Broadway"?
A. "I've never driven a Cadillac"
B. "I've never searched for a ghost"
C. "I've never seen the inside of a factory"
D. "I've never started a fire"

Q80. Which year did Bruce headline Glastonbury Music Festival?
A. 2003
B. 2005

C. 2007
D. 2009

Here is the latest set of answers.

A71. Bruce Springsteen's autobiography is titled "Born to Run". Not published until 2016, this memoir offers an in-depth look at Springsteen's life, from his early years in New Jersey to his rise as one of the most influential musicians in rock history.

A72. Bruce opened the Super Bowl XLIII halftime show with "Tenth Avenue Freeze-Out" and he followed it with Born to Run, Working on a Dream and finished the 12-minute set with Glory Days. The performance was energetic and showcased his dynamic stage presence, making it one of the most memorable halftime shows in history.

A73. "Darkness on the Edge of Town" was released first in 1978. Nebraska was released in 1982, Tunnel of Love in 1987 and The Rising in 2002. "Darkness on the Edge of Town" was a critical and commercial success, continuing to solidify Bruce's reputation as a major artist in rock music.

A74. The album "Magic" was released in September 2007. The album was the fifteenth studio album of Bruce's career, and it marked a return to the E Street Band's classic sound, featuring a mix of energetic rock and introspective ballads.

A75. The album "Wrecking Ball" was released in 2012. This album includes politically charged lyrics and reflects Springsteen's response to economic hardships and social issues.

A76. Bruce sold the rights to his music in 2021 to Sony Music Entertainment, owners of the Columbia Records label, for a reported $550 million dollars. It proves he is an astute businessman as well as an incredible musician.

A77. The album "Nebraska" begins with "Nebraska" which is based on the real-life story of 19-year-old spree killer Charles Starkweather. The song's narrative explores themes of law enforcement and familial loyalty in the context of Starkweather's criminal activities.

A78. John Lyon has never been a member of the E Street Band. The other three musicians mentioned have all been members of the E Street Band at some point in their careers.

A79. In his stage show "Springsteen on Broadway", Bruce said, "I've never seen the inside of a factory and yet it's all I've ever written about. Standing before you is a man who has become wildly and absurdly successful writing about something of which he has had absolutely no personal experience."

A80. During the 2009 Working on a Dream Tour, Bruce headlined Glastonbury, and put on one of his best ever live performances. The three-hour set breached the site curfew by 15 minutes, but the festival organisers were more than happy to pay the huge fines for such a great show.

Here is the next set of questions, this time on lyrics within a song.

Q81. Which song contains the lyrics "The highway's jammed with broken heroes on a last chance power drive"?
A. Backstreets
B. Born to Run
C. Racing in the Street
D. Thunder Road

Q82. Which song features the line "The hungry and the hunted explode into rock'n'roll bands that face off against each other out in the street"?
A. Hungry Heart
B. Jungleland
C. Rosalita
D. Streets of Philadelphia

Q83. Which song includes the line "End up like a dog that's been beat too much, till you spend half your life just covering up"?
A. Because the Night
B. Born in the U.S.A.
C. Secret Garden
D. The River

Q84. Which song contains the lyrics "But I remember us riding in my brother's car, her body tan and wet, down at the reservoir"?
A. Badlands
B. Racing in the Street
C. The River

D. Thunder Road

Q85. Which song contains the lyrics "I walked the avenue, 'til my legs felt like stone, I heard the voices of friends vanished and gone"?
A. Fade Away
B. Glory Days
C. Streets of Philadelphia
D. Tenth Avenue Freeze-Out

Q86. Which song features the line "The road is dark, and it's a thin, thin line, but I want you to know, I'll walk it for you any time"?
A. Blinded by the Light
B. Cover Me
C. I'm on Fire
D. Tougher Than the Rest

Q87. Which song features the line "In the end, what you don't surrender, well, the world just strips away"?
A. Better Days
B. Human Touch
C. Lucky Town
D. The Rising

Q88. Which song features the line "You sit around getting older, there's a joke here somewhere and it's on me"?
A. Brilliant Design
B. Dancing in the Dark
C. Thunder Road
D. Tunnel of Love

Q89. Which song contains the lyrics "Families sleeping in the cars in the south west, no home, no job, no peace, no res"?
A. Backstreets
B. Land of Hope and Dreams
C. The Ghost of Tom Joad
D. War

Q90. Which song includes the lyrics "Think I'm going down to the well tonight and I'm gonna drink 'til I get my fill"?
A. Better Days
B. Glory Days
C. Lonesome Day
D. My Lucky Day

Here are the answers to the lyrics round of questions.

A81. The lyrics "The highway's jammed with broken heroes on a last chance power drive" are of course from "Born to Run". This iconic song captures the sense of longing and escape that defines much of Springsteen's early work.

A82. The line "The hungry and the hunted explode into rock'n'roll bands that face off against each other out in the street" is from "Jungleland". It is an epic ten-minute anthem about the beauty of everyday life in blue-collar New Jersey. It features a fantastic saxophone solo and is a crowd favorite at Springsteen's concerts.

A83. The line "You end up like a dog that's been beat too much, till you spend half your life just covering up" is from "Born in the U.S.A.".

A84. "But I remember us riding in my brother's car, her body tan and wet, down at the reservoir" is from "The River". The song reflects themes of struggle and resilience, portraying the challenges of working-class life.

A85. "But I remember us riding in my brother's car, her body tan and wet, down at the reservoir" is from "Streets of Philadelphia". The song captures a sense of loneliness and longing, with memories of friends who are no longer around.

A86. The line "The road is dark, and it's a thin, thin line, but I want you to know, I'll walk it for you any time" is from "Tougher Than the Rest". This track is known for its straightforward lyrics and classic rock sound, exploring themes of love and resilience.

A87. The line "In the end, what you don't surrender, well, the world just strips away" is from "Human Touch". This song suggests that life's hardships forces us to let go of things we try to hold onto, highlighting the power of external forces over our lives.

A88. The line "You sit around getting older, there's a joke here somewhere and it's on me" is from "Dancing in the Dark". The song reflects themes of dissatisfaction and searching for meaning, delivered with an upbeat melody.

A89. The lyrics "Families sleeping in the cars in the south west, no home, no job, no peace, no rest" are from "The Ghost of Tom Joad". This song reflects Springsteen's exploration of various social issues.

A90. The lyrics "Think I'm going down to the well tonight and I'm gonna drink 'til I get my fill" are from "Glory Days". This song is a nostalgic anthem reflecting on the fleeting nature of youth, and the way people hold onto memories of better times.

OK, here goes with the final set of questions. Enjoy!

Q91. How many Grammy Awards has Bruce won?
A. 5
B. 10
C. 15
D. 20

Q92. Which year did Bruce win his first Grammy award?
A. 1981
B. 1985
C. 1987
D. 1989

Q93. Which year did Bruce win his last Grammy award?
A. 2010
B. 2014
C. 2018
D. 2022

Q94. Which year did Bruce win an Academy Award for Best Original Song?
A. 1992
B. 1994
C. 1996
D. 1998

Q95. Which year did Bruce win a Golden Globe Award for Best Original Song for "The Wrestler"?
A. 2003
B. 2005

C. 2007
D. 2009

Q96. When was Bruce presented with The Presidential Medal of Freedom?
A. 1986
B. 1996
C. 2006
D. 2016

Q97. When was Bruce inducted into the Rock and Roll Hall of Fame?
A. 1990
B. 1993
C. 1996
D. 1999

Q98. What album cover features a red baseball cap sticking out of the pocket of a pair of blue jeans?
A. Born in the U.S.A.
B. Hungry Heart
C. The Rising
D. Tunnel of Love

Q99. What is Bruce's best-selling single of all time?
A. Born to Run
B. Dancing in the Dark
C. Hungry Heart
D. Streets of Philadelphia

Q100. What is Bruce's best-selling album of all time?
A. Born in the U.S.A.
B. Born to Run

C. The River
D. Tunnel of Love

Q101. What are Bruce Springsteen's fans commonly called?
A. Springsteeners
B. Springsteenistas
C. The Boss Squad
D. The E Street Nation

Here is the final set of answers.

A91. Bruce has won 20 Grammy Awards. His Grammy wins reflect his significant impact on the music industry and his ability to connect deeply with people of all ages.

A92. Bruce won his first Grammy Award in 1985 for Best Rock Vocal Performance, Male for "Dancing in the Dark".

A93. Bruce won his last Grammy Award in 2010 for Best Solo Rock Vocal Performance for "Working on a Dream."

A94. Bruce won an Academy Award (commonly known as an Oscar) in 2003 for Best Original Song for "Streets of Philadelphia" which he wrote for the movie "Philadelphia".

A95. Bruce won the Golden Globe Award for Best Original Song in 2009 for "The Wrestler." This award recognized the powerful and evocative nature of the song, which was featured in the film of the same name. This was his second Gloden Globe Award, after winning the Award for Best Original Song in 1994 for "Streets of Philadelphia".

A96. Barack Obama presented Bruce with The Presidential Medal of Freedom - the Nation's highest civilian honor - at a glittering ceremony in 2016.

A97. Bruce was inducted into the Rock and Roll Hall of Fame in 1999. This recognition acknowledged his exceptional career and lasting influence on the music industry.

A98. The album cover for "Born in the U.S.A." shows Springsteen standing against the stripes of an American flag. He is wearing a white T-shirt and jeans, with a red baseball cap sticking out of his right back pocket. The cover photograph was taken by celebrated photographer Annie Leibovitz.

A99. Bruce's best-selling single is "Dancing in the Dark". This song achieved widespread commercial success globally.

A100. Bruce's best-selling album is "Born in the U.S.A." which became one of the best-selling albums of all time and has sold over 30 million copies worldwide.

A101. Bruce Springsteen's fans are commonly referred to as "The E Street Nation". This nickname reflects the close connection and loyalty of his fanbase, named after his famous backing band, the E Street Band.

That's a great question to finish with.

That's it. I hope you enjoyed this book, and I hope you got most of the answers right. I also hope you learnt some new things about Bruce!

If you have any comments or if you saw anything wrong, please email support@glowwormpress.com and we'll get the book updated. We have updated the book thanks to other fans, and we do read every email.

There is just one thing left to do if you'd be so kind, and that's to leave a positive review on Amazon.

Many thanks in advance.

Printed in Great Britain
by Amazon